Activities for 3-5 year olds

Gardening

 Brilliant Publications Caroline Quin & Sue Pearce

We hope you enjoy using this book. If you would like further information on other titles published by Brilliant Publications, please write to the address given below.

Note: to avoid the clumsy 'he/she', the child is referred to throughout as 'she'.

Published by Brilliant Publications, The Old School Yard, Leighton Road, Northall, Dunstable, Bedfordshire LU6 2HA

Written by Caroline Quin and Sue Pearce
Illustrated by Frank Endersby

Printed in Malta by Interprint Limited

© Caroline Quin and Sue Pearce
ISBN 1 897675 40 2

First published 1998
10 9 8 7 6 5 4 3 2 1

Contents

Introduction

Gardening gives children a wealth of knowledge, skills and experiences. It offers opportunities to grow and care for seeds and plants, and to observe and record how they grow and discover, perhaps, why they didn't grow!

The activities are organized to work within the framework of QCA's Desirable Learning Outcomes and take into account the child's developing intellectual, social and physical skills, focusing upon ideas that will encourage the growth of a positive self-image and a positive attitude to those around her.

Try to adopt a 'play' approach as much as possible, and be flexible. Whatever the focus of any activity, the child will be learning all kinds of things from it and much will depend on your starting point. Always start from what the children already know, and their interests. You should be able to adapt all the activities in this book to work with either individual children or a small group, without too much problem.

When using this book you will need to plan ahead. It may be useful to write notes on a calendar, so that you are prepared and can give the children the best opportunities to see the results of their work. It is particularly necessary to be mindful of the sowing, growing and harvesting times of any plants grown.

Use buckets, tubs, window boxes, or similar strong containers – they are more versatile than planting straight into the garden soil, but do allow the children to dig, hoe, rake and sieve any outside plot of garden area. You can purchase proper child-sized gardening tools now at some garden centres. For schools or groups without a suitable outside area, many of the activities can be easily carried out inside.

Where possible, when your food crops are ready, plan to include in cookery the foods that the children have grown.

It is extremely important when gardening and using soil from outside to observe stringent hygiene practices. Where possible use clean soil – if necessary purchase the appropriate type from a garden centre. You also need to be fully aware of what plants, shrubs, berries, etc are poisonous or likely to cause allergic reactions when touched or ingested. Discuss your plans with a garden centre if you are uncertain.

A close look

What children should learn

Language and literacy – to look closely at what they observe and to talk about it.

What you need

Bug boxes (small enclosed boxes with magnifying lids); magnifying glasses; leaves; stones; flowers; mosses; ferns; woodlice; earwigs, etc; plain paper to use as a background.

Activity

Work with groups of about three children. Carefully place the woodlice, earwigs, etc in the enclosed bug boxes. Put them on a table together with the inanimate items and the magnifying glasses.

Look at the creatures yourself so that you can discuss them with the children. Suggest that they put the leaves, flowers and stones on the plain paper so they are not distracted by the grain of the table. Let the children look at the creatures and the leaves, flowers and stones. Encourage them to talk about what they see.

Extension

Let the children draw what they have observed. Suggest that they look at their fingers and study their fingerprints. Let the children help you to release the creatures carefully outside after the activity is finished.

Talk about

Discuss how much more detail can be seen under a magnifying glass. Can they see how many legs the creatures have? Do they have feelers or wings? Can they see the veins on the leaves? That is where the sap goes through. Can they see the striations on a stone?

Leaf shadows

What children should learn

Language and literacy – to recognize the differing shapes of leaves (as a precursor to recognizing letter shapes).

What you need

A large variety of the same and different leaves; spray paint; face masks (can be bought from any large decorating store); sugar paper or other paper of a reasonable weight; Blu-tack.

Activity

Carry out this activity one to one, in the open on a still day or in a separate room. Explain to the child that she is going to attach some leaves to the paper and why she must wear a mask. Do not tell her what the end result will be. Let the child select a number of leaves and fix them to the sugar paper with tiny bits of Blu-tack. Talk about the different shapes of the leaves. Has she chosen any leaves that are the same shape? Can she find any leaves similar to the ones she has chosen in the pile of leaves on the table? Both wearing masks, let the child spray all over the paper and the leaves. Allow to dry for a few minutes (spray paint dries very quickly), then pull the leaves off the paper.

Extension

Older or more able children may want to make a pattern or design with their leaves. At celebration times spray with gold or silver paint.

Talk about

While waiting for the paint to dry, ask the child what she thinks she will get when the leaves are pulled off the paper. Can she remember why she chose the leaves that she sprayed?

Smells and tastes

What children should learn

Language and literacy – to name the smells and tastes that they encounter.

What you need

Yoghurt pots; gauze, fine cotton (or something similar to cover them); elastic bands; some different smells and tastes from the garden (eg cut-up onion, mint, lavender, fresh basil, fresh thyme, bruised strawberries, stewed apple and blackberry, cucumber etc); similar pots of all the edible items, covered over with a tea-towel; spoons; water to drink.

Activity

Check that none of the children has allergies to any of the things you plan to use. Working one to one, ask the child to smell each pot. Can she tell what is in the pot? Does she think she has smelt it before? Give her clues such as 'this goes with new potatoes' for mint, or 'some people like these with cream' for strawberries. Ask her to tell you what the smells are or what they remind her of.

Next let her taste the tasting pots. Reassure her that you will give her just a tiny bit. Let her swallow some water between each tasting. Taste them yourself to show they are all right. Ask similar questions.

Extension

Ask the children to match pictures of the items with the tastes and smells they noted. (Make sure the children cannot see the pictures until after the activity, in order not to give them 'clues'.)

Talk about

Did the tastes taste like the smells? (Basil does not.) Was the child able to recognize the smells and tastes? Remind the child that not everything is safe to taste and that she should ask an adult if she is not sure about whether something is safe.

Talking about gardens

What children should learn

Language and literacy – to participate in a small group discussion and increase their vocabulary.

What you need

Some pictures of gardens, including if possible some of your own garden.

Activity

Work with a small group of children. Show the children pictures of the gardens and discuss what is in them. Try to ensure that the children all get a chance to join in the discussion. Ask open-ended questions to help to develop their imagination and ability to speculate. Does everybody have a garden? What do they have in their gardens – plants? What sort – flowers or vegetables? Do they have trees, garden toys such as a swing or climbing frame, a shed, a greenhouse or a pond? What about people who live in flats? Do they always have gardens? What about those who live in houseboats? What happens if old people or people with disabilities can't manage to do their gardening?

Extension

Provide an interest table of gardening tools, seed packets, etc. Tell the children that the science of gardening is called horticulture.

Talk about

Do their gardens have a lawn? Who cuts the lawn? What other jobs need to be done in the garden? What is a weed? Who in their family does most of the work in the garden?

Above or below

What children should learn

Mathematics – to group vegetables that grow above or below the ground.

What you need

A variety of vegetables: potatoes, carrots, swedes, turnips, parsnips, cauliflower, brussel sprouts, runner beans, cabbage, peas in pods, broccoli, courgettes, onions, broad beans, lettuce, beetroot, radishes (try to provide some less usual vegetables such as sweet potatoes, capsicum, asparagus, marrow and squash); large trays or tin lids (or circles drawn with chalk).

Activity

Place all the vegetables on the table in a haphazard manner, together with two large trays or tin lids. Ask the children to divide the vegetables into two groups: those that grow above the ground and those that grow below. Encourage them to look for clues. For example, can they see roots on any of the vegetables? Do any of them have lots of dirt on them? Are there leaves attached to any of them? Do leaves grow underground?

Extension

Ask the children to decide on another way of grouping the vegetables, eg by size. Some of the vegetables can be washed and cut up afterwards and made into soup. Others can be cooked to show the difference between the raw and cooked state.

Talk about

Discuss other ways the vegetables can be sorted: by colour, by whether you have to peel them or not, those used in salad, etc. Talk about the different, less usual vegetables. Which vegetables do the children like to eat?

Garden beasts

What children should learn

Mathematics – to count the different varieties of insects and other creatures they find in the garden.

What you need

Pencil; paper; clipboard; books from which to identify the creatures.

Activity

In small groups (with an adult per group), go out into the garden and see what insects / creatures you can find. Record where you find them. Count the number of different types you find and how many of each type. Do not move the creatures from their habitats. Ensure the children do not touch the creatures, and see that they wash their hands when they go indoors.

You could expect to find snails, slugs, caterpillars, moths, ants, butterflies, ladybirds, bees, wasps, earwigs, woodlice, beetles, spiders, grasshoppers, and others. You may not necessarily find all these creatures at the same time of year, so this activity can be carried out at different times of the year to compare the seasons.

Extension

Do this in separate groups at different times, allowing each group the same amount of time and compare who found the most.

Talk about

Can the children name the creatures that were found? Explain that insects have Latin names that are common across the world so that all scientists can know exactly what they are talking about. For example, butterflies are *Lepidoptera*, and bees are *Hymenoptera*.

Pressed flowers

What children should learn

Mathematics – to gain a sense of time as they wait for the flowers to dry and press completely.

What you need

A calendar with clear dates; a variety of flowers, leaves and weeds (not thick-stemmed ones like carnations or dandelions); blotting paper; a commercial flower press or weighty books under which to press the flowers; a flat surface or a tray to store the flowers while they press; some already pressed flowers to show the children.

Activity

Mark the date on the calendar on which you begin to press the flowers and mark the date you will open them up (you should leave about six weeks).

Let each child choose the flowers she wants to press and lay them out on the blotting paper, evenly spaced and not touching. Place another piece of blotting paper across the top and put a good weight on them. Place them on a flat surface or on a tray.

Mark each day off on the calendar. At the end of the time, unveil the pressed flowers.

Extension

Make collages, cards or calendars with the flowers when they are completely pressed.

Talk about

Talk about how long it takes for the flowers to dry out and press. What happens to the pressed flowers? Why do some flowers press more successfully than others? Why might a dandelion not press as well as a daisy? Compare the pressed flowers with the original flowers. Are the pressed flowers as bright?

Weighing soil

What children should learn

Mathematics – that soil is heavier than compost and that wet soil is even heavier.

What you need

Clean garden soil; potting compost; water; measuring jugs; four pots such as margarine tubs (identical in size); balancing scales; spoons or trowels.

Activity

Fill one margarine tub with soil and place it on one side of the scales. Fill an identical tub with potting compost and place it on the other side. Which is heavier? Fill two more margarine tubs with soil and compost, but this time add the same amount of water to each. Compare the weight of the tub with water and soil to that with just soil. Which is the heavier tub? Why does adding water make the compost heavier?

Extension

Squeeze the water from the compost. Can they squeeze the water from the soil? Mix the compost and soil together and plant something in it.

Talk about

Discuss how the soil and the compost feel. Which breaks up more easily in the hand? Which do they predict will be lighter?

Feed the birds

What children should learn

Personal and social development – to care for living creatures.

What you need

Separate small pots (such as margarine tubs) to hold the individual ingredients; fromage frais tubs to hold completed bird cakes; string; small mixing bowls; teaspoons; dessertspoons for mixing; as much as possible of the following: minced bacon rind, tiny pieces of bread, raisins, sultanas, chopped apple, peanuts (not salted), cake crumbs, oatmeal; melted fat (eg margarine, lard or dripping, or a combination of these); access to a refrigerator (optional).

Activity

Check that none of the children has an allergy to peanuts. Place all the ingredients except the melted fat in separate margarine tubs on the table with a teaspoon in each bowl. Give each child a small mixing bowl. Let them spoon a small quantity of as many of the ingredients as they choose into their mixing bowl and stir very well until mixed.

Add some cooled melted fat and pack into the fromage frais pots. Allow to cool thoroughly and set (putting them in a refrigerator helps). Cut the bottoms off the fromage frais pots and thread string through the pots and set bird cakes. Hang the bird cakes up for the birds to eat.

Extension

Count the birds which come to eat the cakes in any given period of time. Observe the different species that come.

Talk about

What colour birds can they see? Are they all the same size? Discuss how some birds stay in Britain for winter and others migrate to warmer climates.

Flower arranging

What children should learn

Personal and social development – to make a flower arrangement as a gift.

What you need

Various real flowers (in spring bunches of daffodils can be obtained cheaply); leaves or sprigs (eg from *Cupressus* trees); containers such as tall cream pots; Oasis; water.

Activity

Suggest to the children as they come to the activity that this vase of flowers will be a present for somebody. Ask each child who she will give her flowers to. Is there a special reason to give someone a present? Is it someone's birthday? Has someone done something nice? Is there someone who needs cheering up?

Let the child place some Oasis in a cream pot, then choose a selection of flowers, leaves and twigs to arrange in the Oasis.

Extension

Before embarking on the flower arrangement, paint the cream pots with powder paint mixed with PVA glue. This will not be dry until the next day.

Talk about

Why do people give flowers? Who will they give their flowers to? How / why did they choose the flowers they chose? Why do the flowers need water?

A garden scrapbook

What children should learn

Personal and social development – to contribute to a group project.

What you need

A large scrapbook; pictures of gardens of all types; flowers; vegetables; seed packets.

Activity

To start the scrapbook, use some of the pictures you have supplied. Ask the children to bring in garden pictures to stick in the scrapbook. Tell them the sort of pictures you would like and suggest that they can find them in magazines and seed catalogues. Each time a child brings in a picture, let her stick it in the book and mark it with her name and the date. If a picture is too big, talk over with the child how you are going to fit it into the book: you could fold it, or you could cut it down.

Extension

Make the book accessible in the book corner or on its own table. Look at it with the children. Observe whether the children remember a verbal message to bring in a picture. After a while put a notice out to parents that you need garden pictures.

Talk about

How many pictures are there in the book? Gently remind some children who may have forgotten to bring a picture. Talk about how nice it is to look at the book in the winter as a reminder of the garden in the summer.

Grow a sunflower game

What children should learn

Personal and social development – to wait and take turns when playing a game.

What you need

Die; counters (or buttons); four game cards, prepared as follows: write the numbers 1 – 6 and underneath each number, draw the following (simple illustrations will do):

1   plant pot
2   compost/soil
3   sunflower seeds
4   watering can
5   sprouting plant, with small leaves
6   flowering sunflower.

Activity

Explain the game to the children. Each child takes it in turn to shake the die. They must cover the numbers in order (they cannot get a sprouting plant before they have the compost/soil). Each time a child gets a number, she covers the space with a counter. The first child to complete her card is the winner.

Extension

Leave the game on the table for the children to play with alone. Instead of covering the number with a counter, the children could pick out that number of buttons or counters and place them on their card.

Talk about

Discuss the importance of waiting for one's turn and how the game will only work if the players all play by the rules. Discuss how many other games have rules – from chess to football.

Butterfly prints

What children should learn

Creative development – to make butterfly prints out of mixed paint.

What you need

Sugar paper cut into butterfly shapes (it is best to precut the shapes as the child may feel that her painting is defaced if it is cut afterwards); paint in a variety of colours; brushes or 'squirty' bottles; colourful pictures of butterflies.

Activity

Tell the child she is going to make a butterfly. Ask her to apply paint to one half of the butterfly shape with a brush or a squirty bottle. Squirty bottles require quite a lot of manipulation as too much paint will not produce the required effect. It may be necessary for the child to do several butterflies to find this out for herself. Fold the other half of the paper on top of the painted side and press hard. Peel the paper back and look at the result.

Extension

Leave the butterflies for a day and paint the other side. Hang them as if they are flying. Make smaller versions on card and hang them from metal coat hangers like mobiles.

Talk about

Have you seen any butterflies? What colours have you seen? How big were they? How did they fly? Why do you think you should never touch a butterfly's wings?

Leaf pressings

What children should learn

Creative development – to make impressions of leaves.

What you need

Dough made from equal quantities of salt and plain flour; leaves with strong veins (eg maple or strawberry); rolling pins; silver foil; spare flour.

Activity

Put the dough, rolling pins and clean leaves on a table. Let each child decide how much dough she will need to make her chosen leaf. Roll out the dough into flat squares or rounds on the silver foil (this makes it easier to pick up the finished leaf pressing and put it to one side to dry). Using a rolling pin press the chosen leaf very firmly into the dough until an impression is obtained (sprinkle the leaf with flour if the dough appears a bit wet). Leave the dough tiles to dry in a warm place. The dough will crack if it is dried too rapidly. On top of a radiator, or in an airing cupboard, works well.

Extension

Let each child make her own dough. Paint the leaf impressions, either in 'true to life' colours or in vibrant colours.

Talk about

What colour are leaves? Are they always green? Discuss how leaves are often green when they are on the trees and brown or yellow when they fall off. Have they seen any leaves on trees or plants that are not green? Discuss how the veins run through the leaves and the patterns they make.

Leaf prints

What children should learn

Creative development – to make prints from leaves.

What you need

Paint in a variety of colours; shallow vessels; thin sponges; sugar paper; a lot of clean leaves (cabbage, maple, cherry, nasturtium and iris are nice); protective clothing.

Activity

Put the paint into shallow vessels, with a thin sponge at the bottom. Allow the child to press the leaves gently in the paint and then press them on to the sugar paper to obtain a print. Suggest she tries it with both sides of the leaf. Let her do one or several lots of leaf prints. Ask her whether she wants to make a design on her paper with the leaves.

Extension

Instead of pressing the leaves into the paint, try brushing the paint across the leaf. Let the leaf prints contribute to a wall display.

Talk about

Are the leaves from trees or plants? Cabbages leaves can be eaten. Can any of the other leaves be eaten? Look at the different shapes of the leaves: nasturtium and cabbage are round, iris leaves are long and sword-like. Can you find other leaves of similar shapes?

Miniature gardens

What children should learn

Creative development – to make a small garden in a seed tray.

What you need

Seed trays or similar; potting compost and clean soil (mixed together); a variety of twigs, sticks, leaves, stones, moss, sand, gravel, coloured sweet papers, small flowers (such as daisies and buttercups), silver foil, shells, etc (provide as many things as possible to encourage the children to use their imaginations).

Activity

Show the children how to fill the seed tray about half full with the compost/soil mix and pat it down. Do your own garden while the children are doing theirs. Talk some of the time about what you are doing, eg: 'I think I'll sort out some flat stones to make my path.' Ask them: 'Are you going to have a path?' Let them arrange a garden with the other items provided.

Extension

The children could draw plans of their gardens on paper.

Talk about

What do gardens often have in them – grass, trees, flowers, ponds, fruit, vegetables, etc? Which of these features are they going to put in their gardens?

Scented collage

What children should learn

Creative development – to make a collage of scented herbs from the garden.

What you need

Paper such as sugar paper (cut into about A5 size); PVA glue; a variety of scented herbs fresh from the garden (lavender, basil, lemon verbena, thyme, rosemary, mint, etc).

Activity

Check that none of the children has allergies to any of the things you plan to use. Present all the herbs in separate containers on the table. Suggest the children smell them all before they embark upon making a collage. They will often need to bruise the leaves to get the strongest smell. Fold the paper in half to make a line down the middle and suggest that the child sticks the 'smells' she likes on one side and those she doesn't care for on the other. Alternatively, the child could decide how she was going to divide her smells. Ask her why she made the decision. Leave the collages to dry and then smell them.

Extension

Use dried herbs in addition to, or instead of, the fresh ones. Make pizzas and sprinkle with oregano.

Talk about

Talk about herbs. Which ones can we eat and which ones do we use for other things, eg lavender bags for making sheets smell nice, and mint to go with lamb. Do the children like the smell and taste of the oregano that is usually on pizzas?

Bark rubbings

What children should learn

Physical development – to develop manual dexterity.

What you need

Trees in the garden, park or wood (alternatively, collect pieces of bark); sugar paper; large wax crayons.

Activity

Peel the paper off the crayon. Press the paper against the bark of the tree and rub the side of the crayon across it. Use a number of different trees. Look at the resulting patterns.

Extension

Find a book with pictures of different trees in it and name those trees whose bark you are rubbing. Some trees have very interesting bark, for instance sweet chestnut has a very regular, even pattern. If you are using pieces of bark, make sure you identify the trees from which they came. Name and label the bark.

Talk about

Are the trees in the garden the same trees as those in the parks and woods? Have the children any trees in their gardens? What kinds of trees do they have?

Digging and planting

What children should learn

Physical development – to move and co-ordinate their bodies.

What you need

No special equipment.

Activity

Act out planting potatoes. First of all put on your boots, your anorak and your gardening gloves. Then collect a fork, a rake, a disposal basket, a dibber and the seed potatoes from the shed. Clear away the winter weeds from the patch using a fork. Pull them out – some come out easily, others are very hard to pull out. Throw them in the basket. Dig hard with the fork, turning over the soil. Rake the patch until the soil is fine. Make evenly spaced holes in the patch with the dibber and drop a seed potato in each hole. Rake the earth over the top.

Extension

Let the children make jacket potatoes. Small potatoes, about the size of a medium egg, will cook quite quickly, especially if they are placed on skewers. Let them rub the raw potatoes and dry them on kitchen paper. Cut a cross in the top to allow the air to escape. Bake in the oven for about an hour at gas mark 6/ 400°F/200°C. The potatoes can be eaten at break or taken home.

Talk about

Bring in a selection of potatoes for the children to compare, and discuss the differences. Talk about how many ways potatoes can be cooked.

Planting tomatoes

What children should learn

Physical development – to use the finger and thumb to grip.

What you need

Packets of pelleted tomato seeds; 10 cm plant pots; potting compost; water.

Activity

Each child can plant about three seeds in her pot. Show the children the packets of seed and the pictures on the packets. Tell them that pelleted seeds have a special coating to make them easier to handle. Allow each child to fill her pot with compost, to pinch up three seeds, one at a time, and to plant them evenly spaced across the pot. Water the seeds and put them in a warm place.

Extension

It is likely that two of the resulting plants will have to be pricked out in order for the remaining one to grow successfully. The children can either plant these prickings separately or discard them. Watch the tomato plants grow and water them when necessary. Take out the side shoots. Harvest the tomatoes when they are ready. It will take three to four months from planting to harvest. (The tomato plants may have to go home for the summer holidays.)

Talk about

Explain the reason for pricking out. Talk about the colour of tomatoes. Did the children know that some can be yellow? Talk about the different varieties and show pictures of them.

Bees help plants to grow

What children should learn

Knowledge and understanding of the world – that bees are necessary to pollinate plants.

What you need

Pictures of bees of different kinds; pictures of bee hives and a swarm of bees; a picture of someone in the special clothes worn to collect honey.

Activity

Show the pictures of bees and discuss them with the children. Have they ever seen any bees? Do they know that bees make honey and that bees are very important as they pollinate plants, so that more plants can grow. Explain what 'pollinate' means.

Bees do not sting unless they are provoked, because a bee dies when it stings so it only stings as a last resort to protect itself and other bees. If you are stung by a bee you must not rub the place as the sting can be pulled out (but a wasp does not leave a sting in).

Some bees gather together in swarms. It is thought that bees do something called a 'bee dance' to show the other bees where the best flowers are. The chief bee is called the Queen Bee.

Extension

Make honey sandwiches. Draw pictures of bees.

Talk about

People who keep bees believe that bees are very wise and that any news should be told to the bees, so they go and talk to the bees in their hives. They will tell the bees about such things as the birth of a baby or a wedding. When beekeepers collect the honey they wear special protective clothing.

Garden friends

What children should learn

Knowledge and understanding of the world – that other creatures may share our gardens and that some of them are beneficial to us.

What you need

Pictures of hedgehogs, birds and ladybirds; books about all three.

Activity

Show the pictures to the children and ask if they have seen any of those creatures in their gardens.

Have they ever seen a hedgehog? What happened when they went near it? Did it run away or roll up into a ball? Hedgehogs like to eat slugs. Slugs are not gardeners' friends as they eat the plants the gardener wants to eat or to look nice.

Have they seen any birds' nests in their garden? Do they have a nest box? Birds are good as they eat caterpillars and other insects the gardener wants to keep away.

Have they seen any ladybirds? Ladybirds are good as they eat blackfly and greenfly. Blackfly and greenfly eat the plants that gardeners want to look nice or eat. Ladybirds can have different numbers of spots and be black and yellow, as well as black and red. Ladybirds can fly but they usually keep their wings tucked away.

Extension

Draw pictures of ladybirds, hedgehogs and birds. Hang a bird feeder outside a window where it can be seen by the children. Let the children fill it.

Talk about

Talk about how hedgehogs sleep during the winter. This sleep is called hibernation. Some birds migrate to warmer countries for the winter but some birds stay. Ladybirds disappear in the winter.

Garden in a jar

What children should learn

Knowledge and understanding of the world – to observe plants grown in a garden jar.

What you need

Plastic sweet jars or round fish bowls (you'll need to make a lid for these); clean gravel; barbecue charcoal; potting compost; clean fine soil; dessertspoons and teaspoons (to use as shovels); small house plants such as maidenhair fern or polka dot plant.

Activity

Using your hands or a dessertspoon, thinly layer the gravel, then charcoal, then potting compost and finally a slightly thicker layer of soil in the bottom of the jar (the jar can be upright or laid on its side). Press them down lightly. Using the teaspoon (perhaps tied to a stick to make it easier), plant a couple of plants in the jar. Press the soil down as firmly as possible and water the plants. Put the lid on the jar. If it gets cloudy, take the lid off for a short period. Do not overwater!

Extension

Draw the garden in a jar. Make a graph of how long the plants take to grow. If you have more than one jar, place them in different areas and observe the difference in the growth of the plants.

Talk about

Why does the jar mist up? What colour leaves does your plant have? How are the leaves shaped?

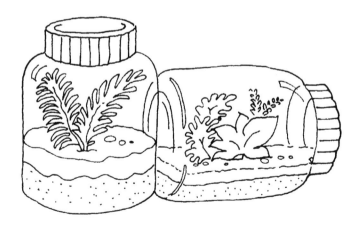

Growing potatoes

What children should learn

Knowledge and understanding of the world – to grow something to eat.

What you need

Early seed potatoes; buckets; a quantity of compost and soil for each bucket; trowels.

Activity

Start this activity at the end of March as the potatoes take about three months to grow. Put a mixture of compost and soil in the bottom of the bucket, and place a few potatoes in it. Cover with more compost/soil. Every time the potatoes sprout above the soil, cover with more soil until just a tiny tip is showing. Keep this up until the bucket is nearly full. When the potatoes have finished flowering, they are ready to harvest. You will get a crop of small potatoes, about the size of table tennis balls.

Extension

Let the children pick the potatoes themselves. Make them into potato salad. Do not peel them.

Talk about

Discuss how long it takes for the potatoes to grow, and how nice it is to eat something you have grown. Ask whether their parents or grandparents grow potatoes.

Growing towards the light

What children should learn

Knowledge and understanding of the world – that plants need light to grow, and that they turn towards a source of light.

What you need

Mustard and cress seeds; potting compost; shallow trays (eg meat trays); water; old shoe boxes.

Activity

Plant the seeds in the compost. Leave them in a warm place to sprout. When they have grown about 1 cm, place some of the seed trays in dark shoe boxes. Do not allow any light to reach them. Place other seed trays in boxes in which a small hole has been cut in the side. Leave the rest of the seed trays to grow normally. Observe what happens to the seedlings on a daily basis (or even more frequently). The seeds in the boxes with a hole in them will lean very markedly towards the light source. Turn the seed trays round during the session and look at them again. The seedlings will be turning again towards the light.

Extension

Record on a graph or chart what happens to the seedlings.

Talk about

Which seedlings grew most quickly and strongly? What happened to the ones with the hole in the box? What does this tell you? What else do plants need in order to grow?

Mini greenhouse

What children should learn

Knowledge and understanding of the world – that seeds and plants grow more rapidly in a warm, moist atmosphere.

What you need

Seeds such as sunflowers and plant cuttings ready to plant (eg busy Lizzie); potting compost; 10 cm plant pots; 2 litre plastic pop bottles (cut in half); trowels or old tablespoons; water.

Activity

Let the children fill the plant pots and plant the seeds or cuttings. Water. Place the half pop bottles over some of the pots to form a mini greenhouse. Explain to the children why you are going to cover some of the pots and leave others uncovered. Otherwise treat all the pots the same: give them the same quantities of water and keep them in the same place, so that they get the same amount of light and heat. Every day observe what has happened to the plants and to the pop bottles.

Extension

Do not water some of the plants, both those covered with pop bottles and those not covered. What happens to these plants? Record on a chart what happens to the plants. Use a house thermometer to take the temperature inside the pots.

Talk about

Which plants have grown the fastest? Why do you think that is? Talk about how plants need warmth to grow and that they grow more rapidly in a warm atmosphere. The pop bottles have a film of condensation on the inside which helps to keep the plants moist.

Dyeing flowers

What children should learn

Knowledge and understanding of the world – that plants 'drink' water and along with it the colour that you have put in the water.

What you need

White or light-coloured flowers, such as carnations and daffodils; several different food colours; vessels for the liquid and to stand the flowers in (clear vessels are best as the children can see the water change when the colour is added).

Activity

Let each child put a quantity of water in a 'vase' vessel. Then let her choose a colour and add at least a teaspoon of food colouring. Encourage the children to watch as they pour the colour in. Let them choose a few flowers and place them in the dyed water. Watch how the petals change colour.

Extension

Try with dark flowers and with leaves. Does the same thing happen? Can you get flowers in colours that they do not normally come in (eg green and black flowers are seldom seen)? This investigation is also very successful with a stick of celery. Time how long it takes for the petals to change colour.

Talk about

Talk about the colour changes. Where is the colour change most apparent? How does the colour change come about?

Roots, roots, roots

What children should learn

Knowledge and understanding of the world – to see how roots develop from plant stems and from seeds.

What you need

Busy Lizzie cuttings; spider plant 'babies'; broad and runner bean and pea seeds; silver foil; jars; sugar paper; scissors; newspaper; water; ruler or spoon.

Activity

Mini jam jars are ideal for this activity, but take extra care when using glass jars. Fill the jars with water. Cover the jars with foil and poke holes in it to hold the cuttings. Push the busy Lizzie cuttings and the spider plant 'babies' through the foil and into the jars. Observe as the plants grow roots.

Line taller glass jars (eg small coffee jars) with sugar paper. The paper will have to be placed below the neck of the jar in order to obtain a tight fit between the paper and the glass and for the beans to be held tightly against the glass. Lightly pack the jar with screwed-up newspaper. Push the beans in between the jar and the paper (you may need a ruler or spoon handle for this). Keep the paper wet, but not soaked.

Extension

Mark off on a calendar how long each different plant takes to make roots. Grow the resulting plants in soil or potting compost. Grow daffodil bulbs in coffee jars (use cocktail sticks to support the bulbs).

Talk about

How long did the roots take to sprout? What are the roots for? It is likely that some of the beans you place will be upside down; see how the roots turn down. Talk about how some of the plants you have grown are edible, and some are not.